Fun Fan Facts:
The Unofficial NBA Edition

Miami Heat

Everything Young Heat
Fans Should Know

By: Jake Liam

Dedication

This one is also for every kid who got told they were too small, too slow, or not quite good enough, and ended up starting for an NBA team anyway. The Heat have built an entire philosophy around proving that wrong, and it works more often than anyone expects.

Miami, this one is yours.

THE NBA BY THE NUMBERS

MOST NBA CHAMPIONSHIPS[*]

- CELTICS (18) [†]
- LAKERS (17)
- WARRIORS (7)
- BULLS (6)
- SPURS (5)

As of the 2024-25 Season. † One Trophy = 4 Championships.

BIG NUMBERS

$156 million
Stephen Curry's est. earnings in the 24-25 season

7'7"
Tallest player in NBA history (Gheorghe Mureșan & Manute Bol)

NBA HISTORY SNAPSHOT

- **1946** NBA Founded
- **1954** Shot Clock Introduced
- **1979** 3-Point Line Added
- **2023** NBA Cup Introduced

30 | 4 | 82

- **30** Teams Competing in the NBA
- **4** Playoff Rounds
- **82** Games Per Season

EASTERN CONFERENCE

- Atlantic – **Celtics**
- Atlantic – **Nets**
- Atlantic – **Knicks**
- Atlantic – **76ers**
- Atlantic – **Raptors**
- Central – **Bulls**
- Central – **Cavaliers**
- Central – **Pistons**
- Central – **Pacers**
- Central – **Bucks**
- Southeast – **Hawks**
- Southeast – **Hornets**
- Southeast – **Heat**
- Southeast – **Magic**
- Southeast – **Wizards**

WESTERN CONFERENCE

- Pacific – **Lakers**
- Pacific – **Clippers**
- Pacific – **Warriors**
- Pacific – **Suns**
- Pacific – **Kings**
- Northwest – **Nuggets**
- Northwest – **Timberwolves**
- Northwest – **Thunder**
- Northwest – **Trail Blazers**
- Northwest – **Jazz**
- Southwest – **Mavericks**
- Southwest – **Rockets**
- Southwest – **Spurs**
- Southwest – **Pelicans**
- Southwest – **Grizzlies**

MIAMI HEAT IN THE NBA

- FOUNDED: 1988[†]
- NBA TITLES: 3
- CONFERENCE TITLES: 7[*]

4 Consecutive NBA Finals (2011–2014)

*† Founding dates are complicated & may cause arguments at Thanksgiving. Ask someone born before color TV. All Titles reflect pre-relocation franchise history. * As of 2024-25 Season.*

NBA ALL-TIME MVP LEADERS

KAREEM ABDUL-JABBAR (6) ★ MICHAEL JORDAN (5) ★ BILL RUSSELL (5)

Introduction

Welcome, fans! Whether you're new to cheering for the Miami Heat or you've been bleeding the team colors your whole life, this book is packed with fun, exciting facts about your favorite team. Get ready to impress your friends and family with everything you know about the Heat.

Quick Time Out

This book is packed with stats. Like, A LOT of stats. Every fact was checked, double-checked, and triple-checked. But here's the thing about basketball history: not everyone agrees on everything. Ask someone who watched games before color TV and someone who grew up with instant replay and you'll get two completely different answers. My dad, stepdad, uncle, and grandpa all argued about the same fact. Four people. Four answers. All of them think they're right. So if you spot something that doesn't match what you've heard, congratulations. You might be a bigger fan than the people who helped make this book. And honestly? That's pretty cool.

HOW IT WORKS

THE SEASON

82 Games. One Goal.

Each team plays 82 games.
Win enough to make the
Playoffs.
Every game counts!

PLAYOFFS

30 Teams. 16 Make It.

8 per conference make the playoffs.
Win=Advance | Lose=Go Home
Best record
gets home court!

PLAYOFF ROUNDS

Best of 7. Win 4 or Go Home.

4 rounds of pure pressure.
Every series is do-or-die!

OVERTIME?

5 More Minutes.

Keep playing until
someone pulls ahead.
No ties. Ever.

THE FINALS

One Series. One Champion.

Winner lifts the Trophy.
Legend status unlocked.

How the NBA Works

At first glance, basketball feels simple. Ten players. One ball. Two hoops. Go.

Then the NBA adds the layers.

An 82-game regular season. A draft where bad teams pick first. Playoffs that last two full months. Superstars who can change everything with one trade. Dynasties that rise, fall, and rise again.

And somehow, it all works.

The NBA is built on one big idea: every team gets a chance to reset, reload, and rise again. No relegation. No dropping down to a lower league. Just basketball, every night, from October through June.

It is a league designed for drama, stars, and comebacks. And once you understand the flow, it is impossible to stop watching.

The League Setup

The NBA has 30 teams, spread across the United States and Canada. Those teams are split into two conferences:

- Eastern Conference
- Western Conference

Each conference has three divisions, mostly based on geography. Divisions matter for scheduling, but not as much as they used to.

Every team plays 82 regular season games, usually from October through April. Home games. Road games. Back-to-back nights. Long road trips. The season is a marathon before the sprint even starts.

Win games, and you climb the standings. Lose too many, and the pressure builds fast.

How Games Are Played

An NBA game has four quarters, each lasting 12 minutes. That means 48 minutes of game time, plus timeouts, free throws, and the occasional coach argument that adds another 20 minutes nobody planned for.

Scoring is simple:

- A shot inside the three-point line is worth 2 points
- A shot beyond the arc is worth 3 points
- Free throws are worth 1 point

If the score is tied at the end of regulation, the game goes to overtime, which lasts 5 minutes. Still tied? Another overtime. Keep going until someone wins.

There is a shot clock too. Teams have 24 seconds to take a shot. No standing around. No holding the ball forever. Keep it moving.

The Regular Season Race

The regular season is long for a reason. It tests everything.

Depth. Health. Focus. Patience.

Teams play opponents from both conferences, but they face conference rivals more often. By the end of the season, each conference's top teams have earned their playoff spots the hard way.

The goal is simple: make the playoffs. But there is a twist.

The NBA Cup

In 2023, the NBA added something new to the middle of the season. Something with actual stakes. They called it the In-Season Tournament, now known as the NBA Cup.

It works like this: Every team plays a small group stage during November and December, with special court designs that look like nothing else in basketball. The best teams advance to a knockout round held in Las Vegas.

The winners split a prize pool. Players earn bonus money. And for the first time, a team could lift a trophy before the playoffs even started.

Some fans are still warming up to it. Some players love it. But the moment a team starts treating it seriously and a crowd shows up buzzing in December, it feels like something.

Which, honestly, sounds about right.

The Play-In Tournament

Instead of sending the top eight teams from each conference straight to the playoffs, the NBA added something new. The Play-In Tournament.

Here is how it works:

- Teams ranked 1 through 6 in each conference are safe
- Teams ranked 7 through 10 fight for the final two playoff spots

The 7 and 8 seeds have an advantage. Win once and you are in. Lose and you still get one more shot. The 9 and 10 seeds have to win twice in a row just to earn a first-round matchup.

It turns the end of the season into a sprint. Every game suddenly matters more. Fans love it. Coaches age rapidly.

The NBA Playoffs

Once the playoffs begin, everything tightens.

Sixteen teams enter. Eight from each conference. Every round is a best-of-seven games series. That means the first team to win four games moves on:

- First Round
- Conference Semifinals
- Conference Finals
- NBA Finals

Home-court advantage matters. Crowds get louder. Rotations get shorter. Superstars play heavier minutes. One bad quarter can flip a series. One great performance can define a career.

By the time the NBA Finals arrive in June, only two teams are left. One from the East. One from the West. Four wins away from a championship. Four wins away from history.

The NBA Draft: Hope Begins Here

Here is where the NBA gets clever. Every summer, new players enter the league through the NBA Draft. Teams take turns selecting college players, international stars, and teenagers straight out of high school.

The teams that finished with the worst records get the best odds to pick early through the Draft Lottery. It is not guaranteed, but it gives struggling franchises a real shot at changing their future with one pick.

That means one bad season does not doom you forever. It might actually change everything. Some franchises are rebuilt by a single draft night moment.

Hope shows up wearing a new jersey.

No Relegation. All Pressure.

Unlike many global sports leagues, NBA teams never drop down to a lower league. They always stay in the NBA.

That does not mean there is no pressure.

Fans remember losing seasons. Owners make changes. Coaches get replaced. Players get traded. Every year is a test of direction, patience, and belief.

Stars, Systems, and Showtime

The NBA is famous for its stars. But stars do not win alone.

Teams need chemistry. Coaches need systems. Role players need to deliver on the biggest stages. One injury. One hot streak. One trade deadline deal. Any of it can flip a season.

That balance between individual brilliance and team basketball is what makes the league special.

Fast breaks. Buzzer-beaters. Game 7s. And moments that get replayed forever. That is the NBA.

Once you get the flow, it is pure electricity.

Miami Heat Facts

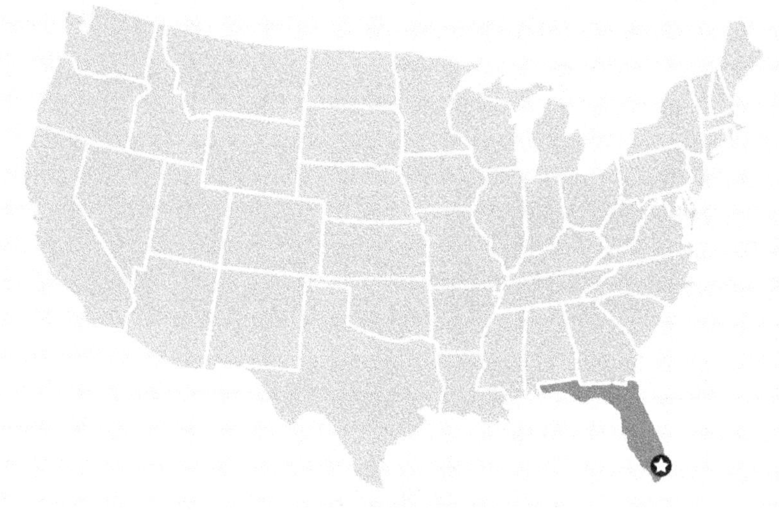

Home City

Miami, Florida

Metro Area Population

About 6.2 Million

Home Arena

Kaseya Center

Arena Capacity

19,600

Conference / Division

Eastern Conference / Southeast Division

Famous Local Food

Cuban Sandwiches, Stone Crab Claws, Pastelitos,
Plantains

Chapter 1: How the Heat Got Hot

1. Miami Gets a Team: Starting From Zero (1988)

In 1988, the NBA decided to expand into four new cities. Miami was one of them. The city got a franchise, a name, and basically nothing else. No history. No banners. No Hall of Famers waiting in the locker room. Just an expansion team starting from scratch in a city better known for beaches and sunshine than basketball arenas.

The Miami Heat paid 32.5 million dollars for the right to exist as an NBA franchise, which sounds like a bargain until you realize what they got for it. Their first roster was built through an expansion draft, which meant every other team in the league got to protect their good players first and hand Miami whatever was left over. It is the basketball equivalent of being the last kid picked at recess, except the recess has 23 other kids who have already decided you are not getting anyone useful.

Their first season went about as well as you would expect. The Heat won 15 games and lost 67. Fifteen. The math on that is brutal. But every franchise has to start somewhere. The Celtics were bad before Bill Russell. The Warriors struggled before Curry. Miami was bad before they figured out who they were. The difference is what happened next, and what happened next was one of the most interesting rebuilds, or just builds, in NBA history.

2. Pat Riley Walks In and Nothing Is Ever the Same (1995)

In 1995, Pat Riley left the New York Knicks to become the head coach and team president of the Miami Heat. This was a significant moment. Riley had already won four championships with the Los Angeles Lakers in the 1980s and had turned the Knicks into one of the toughest, most physical teams in the Eastern Conference. He did not arrive in Miami looking for a vacation. He arrived looking for another ring.

Riley brought with him a coaching philosophy that was not warm or fuzzy. He believed in conditioning, discipline, and defensive toughness. His practices were notoriously demanding. His expectations were high and non-negotiable. Players who wanted an easy ride chose other teams. Players who wanted to be pushed until they figured out what they were actually capable of fit right in.

The results came quickly. Miami made the playoffs in Riley's first season. They built a reputation as a hard team to play against, physically tough and organizationally stable. Pat Riley also had a talent for personal style that became almost as famous as his coaching. He showed up to press conferences in perfectly tailored suits with his hair slicked back, looking like he had just stepped out of a magazine. He looked the part of a winner before his team had won anything in Miami. Sometimes confidence is its own statement.

3. The Rivalry That Gave the Heat Its Edge: Miami vs. New York

The Miami Heat built a lot of their early identity through conflict, and their most important conflict was with the New York Knicks. In the mid-1990s, these two teams met in the playoffs four times in five years, and every single series was physical, intense, and occasionally something your parents probably did not want you watching.

The Knicks were coached by Pat Riley before he left for Miami, which meant Riley knew exactly how New York played and the Knicks knew exactly how Miami would play. Both teams played brutally tough defense. Both teams fouled hard. Both teams had players who genuinely did not like each other. It made for compelling basketball if you were a fan and exhausting basketball if you were a referee.

The rivalry did something important for the Heat beyond the wins and losses. It gave Miami an identity. They were not a finesse team that tried to outscore you. They were a team that tried to make you uncomfortable for 48 minutes and wear you down until you made mistakes. That identity, built in the trenches of those Knicks series in the late 1990s, became the foundation of everything that followed. Toughness was not just a strategy for the Heat. It became a brand.

4. Dwyane Wade Arrives: The Draft Pick That Changed Miami (2003)

In the summer of 2003, the Miami Heat had the fifth pick in the NBA Draft. There was enormous attention that year on the first pick, a high school kid from Akron, Ohio, named LeBron James. And the second pick. And the third and fourth. By the time Miami was on the clock, most of the conversation had moved on. Then they picked Dwyane Wade out of Marquette University, and the Heat's future arrived quietly through the side door.

Wade had not been a heavily recruited high school player. Marquette took a chance on him when bigger programs passed. He developed into one of the best players in college basketball and came into the NBA with something that does not show up in scouting reports: a competitive instinct that made him better in big moments than in small ones. The brighter the lights, the better Wade played. That trait would prove useful.

In his rookie season Wade averaged 16.2 points per game and immediately looked like someone who belonged. He was quick, creative, and defensively sharp in a way that young players often are not. The Heat had their cornerstone. They just needed to build around him, which they were about to do in a very dramatic fashion.

5. Shaq Comes to South Beach: The Big Arrival (2004-2008)

In the summer of 2004, the Miami Heat traded for Shaquille O'Neal. Shaq was three championships deep with the Los Angeles Lakers, a four-time MVP, and one of the most physically dominant players the NBA had ever seen. He was also, at that point, in a very public and very messy falling out with his Laker teammate Kobe Bryant. The Lakers chose Kobe. Miami got Shaq.

Putting Shaquille O'Neal next to Dwyane Wade was an interesting experiment in contrasts. Shaq was 32 years old, seven feet tall, and approximately the size of a small vehicle. Wade was 22, six foot four, and built like someone who took the stairs two at a time. One played through brute force. One played through speed and improvisation. Together they formed one of the more unlikely and effective partnerships the league had seen in years.

The city of Miami noticed immediately. Heat tickets became harder to get. The arena got louder. South Beach had always been a place where celebrities showed up, and now NBA celebrities were showing up in a Heat uniform. Shaq brought star power that the franchise had never had before. More importantly, he brought something else with him: a championship pedigree. He had done this before. He knew what it took. And he was about to show his young teammate exactly how it was done.

6. Dwyane Wade: The Heart of the Heat (2003-2019)

There is a version of NBA history where Dwyane Wade is considered the most important player in Miami Heat history. There is also a version where he is second behind a player we will get to shortly. Both arguments are reasonable. What is not debatable is that no player has meant more to the city of Miami, worn the Heat uniform longer, or carried the franchise through more of its defining moments than Dwyane Wade.

Wade spent most of sixteen seasons with the Heat, with brief stops in Cleveland and Chicago sandwiched in between. He won three championships. He was a thirteen-time All-Star. He won a Finals MVP award in 2006 at 24 years old, putting on one of the best individual performances in Finals history. He was the kind of player who made the difficult look routine and the impossible look merely difficult.

What made Wade special beyond the numbers was the way he played. He attacked the basket with a combination of power and creativity that defenders struggled to plan for. He could absorb contact, finish through it, and get to the free throw line at a rate that made opposing coaches frustrated. He was also a better defender than he ever got credit for, making three All-Defensive teams during his career. When Wade retired in 2019 with the Heat, the arena gave him a sendoff that said everything about what he meant to that building and that city.

Dwyane Wade hanging on the rim after another Miami Heat slam. Speed to the basket. Boom at the rim. "Flash" made defenders nervous every time he attacked the paint. *Photo: Dwyane Wade hanging on the rim. Photograph by Keith Allison. Licensed under CC BY-SA 2.0. Source: Wikimedia Commons.*

7. LeBron James: The Decision and the Four Years That Followed (2010-2014)

In the summer of 2010, LeBron James was a free agent. He had spent seven seasons in Cleveland, dragged that team to the Finals almost by himself in 2007, and decided it was time to find teammates who could help him win a championship. What happened next became one of the most talked about moments in sports that had nothing to do with an actual game.

LeBron announced his decision to join the Miami Heat in a televised special called The Decision. He was joining Dwyane Wade and Chris Bosh, forming a trio that had been assembled in secret over months of planning. The reaction was enormous and not entirely positive. Cleveland fans burned his jersey. Critics called it a shortcut. The basketball world split into camps. Whatever you thought about how it happened, the result was one of the most talented rosters the league had assembled in years.

Miami went to four consecutive Finals with LeBron. They won two championships, in 2012 and 2013. LeBron won two Finals MVP awards and was the best player in the world during his time on South Beach. He left for Cleveland in 2014, which stung. But what he left behind was a two-year window of basketball that Heat fans still talk about with something close to reverence. The four years were complicated, loud, occasionally messy, and absolutely worth it.

8. Shaquille O'Neal: One Ring, One Era, One Giant (2004-2008)

We covered Shaq's arrival in Chapter 1, but his time in Miami deserves a closer look because it was both shorter and more impactful than most people remember. Shaq spent four seasons with the Heat, won one championship, and left a fingerprint on the franchise that never fully faded.

By the time Shaq arrived in Miami he was no longer the unstoppable force he had been in Los Angeles, but he was still one of the most effective centers in the league when healthy. He averaged 22.9 points and 10.4 rebounds in his first Heat season. He knew how to set screens that opened up space for Wade. He knew how to seal defenders in the post and make the simple play. After years of being the center of every offense he played in, Shaq adjusted his game in Miami to make room for a younger star. That flexibility is underrated in the story of his career.

The 2006 championship run was the peak. Shaq was 34 years old and still capable of taking over games when the moment called for it. He and Wade made a genuinely difficult team to beat. After the title, injuries slowed him down significantly. He was traded to Phoenix in 2008 before his contract expired. Four seasons. One ring. Enough memorable moments to fill a highlight reel that runs for an hour. That is not a bad return on a gamble.

9. Alonzo Mourning: The Warrior Who Never Quit (1995-2008)

Alonzo Mourning was a center who played like every single game was something he needed to win personally. He was six feet ten, built like a piece of construction equipment, and defended the basket with a ferocity that made opposing big men think twice before driving the lane. He came to Miami with Pat Riley in 1995 and became the face of the franchise during its first serious era of relevance.

Mourning was a two-time Defensive Player of the Year. He averaged more than two blocked shots per game for his career, which puts him among the most effective shot-blockers the league has produced. He made six

All-Star teams. He was the kind of player who changed what the other team was willing to attempt just by being on the floor. Layups that were automatic against other teams became risky propositions against Mourning.

Then in 2000, he was diagnosed with a serious kidney disease that threatened not just his career but his life. He missed significant time. He underwent treatment. He came back, left, and eventually returned to Miami one more time to win a championship as a reserve in 2006, playing a supporting role on a team that remembered what he had meant to the franchise for a decade. He received his ring as a backup. Considering everything he had been through to still be standing in that moment, it was one of the more earned rings in NBA history.

10. Chris Bosh: The Most Underrated Champion (2010-2016)

When the Miami Heat assembled their trio in 2010, every conversation was about LeBron James and Dwyane Wade. Chris Bosh flew in somewhat under the radar, which tells you everything you need to know about how good LeBron and Wade were and how underappreciated Bosh consistently was throughout his career.

Bosh was a six-time All-Star who had been the clear number one option in Toronto for six seasons before joining Miami. He averaged 24 points per game in his final year as a Raptor. He was a legitimate star on any other team in the league. In Miami, he became the third option, which meant moving away from the basket, shooting more threes, and doing the less glamorous work that allowed his two teammates to operate. He did all of it without complaint and did it well.

Bosh made 37 percent of his three-pointers during the Heat's championship seasons. For a power forward in the early 2010s, that number was genuinely unusual. Big men did not shoot threes at that rate back then. Bosh's willingness to stretch the floor created driving lanes for Wade and LeBron that would not have existed if Bosh had camped in the paint. His career was cut short by a blood clotting condition that forced him to retire at 32. Two championships, six All-Star appearances, and a legacy that keeps growing the more people look back and understand what he actually contributed.

11. The 2006 Championship: Wade Takes the Wheel

The 2006 NBA Finals matched the Miami Heat against the Dallas Mavericks. Dallas won Game 1 and Game 2. They were up by thirteen points in the fourth quarter of Game 3 before Miami came back to win. From that moment forward, Dwyane Wade turned the series into something that was essentially his personal showcase, and the Mavericks had no reliable answer.

Wade averaged 34.7 points per game in the final four games of the series. He attacked the basket relentlessly, drawing fouls at a rate that kept him at the free throw line in the closing minutes of close games. He made the big shots. He made the right passes when double teams came. At 24 years old, in his third NBA season, he carried Miami to a championship that almost nobody had predicted at the start of the series.

Shaq was the veteran presence and Shaq was important. But that Finals belonged to Wade in a way that cemented his status as one of the genuinely special players of his generation. The Mavericks had been the favorites. Dallas had Dirk Nowitzki, one of the best offensive players in the game. Miami had a 24-year-old who just happened to play his best basketball when the stakes were the highest. The Heat won four straight after going down two games to zero. Wade walked away with the trophy and the Finals MVP. South Beach celebrated for three days.

12. The Big Three: Two Years, Two Rings (2012-2013)

The Miami Heat's Big Three of LeBron James, Dwyane Wade, and Chris Bosh made four consecutive Finals appearances. They lost the first one to Dallas in 2011 in a series that was humbling and educational. Then they won two in a row, beating Oklahoma City in 2012 and San Antonio in 2013, and for those two seasons Miami was the best team in basketball.

The 2012 championship was LeBron's first. He had come to Miami specifically because he wanted to win a ring, and in the 2012 playoffs he delivered the kind of performance that made it impossible to argue against him as the best player in the world. He was dominant in ways that went beyond scoring. He defended multiple positions. He made his teammates better. He controlled the pace of games in ways that do not always show up in the box score.

The 2013 title was even better, if only because of what had to happen to win it. The Heat faced a San Antonio Spurs team that was experienced, disciplined, and absolutely focused on winning. Getting past them required one of the most dramatic games in Finals history, which brings us to the next fact. Back to back championships for any team in the modern NBA is legitimately difficult. The roster management, the health, the sustained focus required over an entire season and postseason. Miami did it twice. That earns respect regardless of what you thought about how the team was assembled.

13. Ray Allen's Corner Three: Twenty Seconds From Losing (2013)

Game 6 of the 2013 NBA Finals. San Antonio leads the series three games to two. The Spurs lead the game by three points with 19 seconds left. Miami has no timeouts. The ball goes up toward the basket, misses, and LeBron James tips it out to the corner where Ray Allen is standing. Allen catches it, his feet already set, his balance already perfect, and releases a three-pointer that ties the game with 5.2 seconds remaining.

Imagine this: you are a Heat fan in the lower bowl of the arena. Your team is three possessions from losing the championship. The Spurs have played nearly perfect basketball for most of six games. You are watching the clock and doing the math and the math is not good. Then the ball kicks out. Then Ray Allen catches it. Then the net moves. Then the building makes a sound you have never heard it make before.

Miami won in overtime. They won Game 7 the next night. They won the championship. Without that shot, the series ends in San Antonio's favor and basketball history reads completely differently. Ray Allen was 37 years old when he made that shot. He had left the Boston Celtics to join Miami specifically because he wanted another ring and thought this team gave him the best chance. He had been criticized for leaving. The corner three in Game 6 is what people remember. One shot. Five seconds left. Everything on the line. It went in.

14. The 2020 Bubble Run: The Team Nobody Expected

In the summer of 2020, the NBA restarted its season inside a protective bubble at the Walt Disney World complex in Orlando, Florida. Every team was isolated. No fans. No home court advantage. Just basketball in a controlled environment while the world outside dealt with a pandemic. Under those unusual circumstances, the Miami Heat did something that almost nobody had predicted.

Miami made the NBA Finals. They did it without a single player who had been an All-Star that season. They did it with a roster built largely on Heat Culture and player development rather than big free agent signings. Jimmy Butler played like a man who had been waiting his entire career for a moment this big, averaging 26 points per game in the bubble playoffs. Bam Adebayo emerged as one of the best two-way players in the league. A second-year player named Tyler Herro scored 37 points in a playoff game off the bench at 20 years old.

They lost the Finals to the Los Angeles Lakers in six games. LeBron, by that point in a Lakers uniform, won his fourth championship. But what Miami showed in those bubble playoffs was the kind of thing that is hard to manufacture. No superstars on paper. No guarantees. A team that played together, believed in each other, and nearly won a championship on effort and identity alone. The 2020 run did not end with a trophy. It ended with a franchise knowing exactly who it was.

15. Bam Adebayo's 83 Points: A Night for the Record Books (2026)

On March 10, 2026, Bam Adebayo scored 83 points for the Miami Heat in a 150-129 win over the Washington Wizards. Eighty-three. In one game. The performance moved him past Kobe Bryant's 81-point game from 2006, which had stood as the second-highest single-game scoring total in NBA history for twenty years, and left him with only Wilt Chamberlain's 100-point game ahead of him.

Adebayo had never scored more than 41 points in a game before that night. He came in averaging 18.9 points per game for the season, which is a solid number for a starting center but not exactly a sign that history was coming. Then he scored 31 in the first quarter alone. By halftime he had 43. By the end of the third quarter he had 62 and the entire basketball world had stopped whatever it was doing.

There was controversy, as there tends to be when records fall in unusual circumstances. The Wizards fouled Heat players down the stretch to stop the clock, and Miami's players funneled the ball back to Adebayo to keep him scoring. Not everyone loved how the final minutes unfolded. But the final number was 83, and no amount of argument changes what it says in the record book. For Heat fans, it was a moment that tied the present directly to the deepest history of the sport. Wilt. Then Bam. Then everyone else. Not bad for a center from Kentucky who most people associated with defense.

16. Heat Culture: What It Actually Means

Heat Culture is a phrase that gets used a lot. It shows up in press conferences and social media posts and player interviews. But it is not just a slogan printed on a T-shirt. It is a specific set of standards that the Miami Heat organization has maintained for thirty years, and it shapes everything from how they draft players to how they run practice to how they decide who stays and who goes.

The basics are this: the Heat expect maximum effort from every player regardless of contract size, roster spot, or reputation. Veteran stars are not exempt from competing for playing time. Young players are expected to earn their minutes rather than receive them based on where they were drafted. Practice intensity is treated as seriously as game intensity. Players who fit those expectations tend to thrive in Miami. Players who do not fit them tend to find themselves somewhere else fairly quickly.

The most visible proof of Heat Culture is what the organization does with undrafted players and low-round picks, which we will cover shortly. But the culture starts at the top with Pat Riley and Erik Spoelstra and runs all the way down to the last man on the roster. It is why players who leave Miami and go to other organizations sometimes come back years later and say the Heat years were the ones that made them professionals. A high standard consistently applied is worth something. Miami applies it consistently.

17. The Undrafted Army: Miami's Secret Weapon

The Miami Heat have developed more undrafted players into legitimate NBA contributors than almost any other franchise in the league. This is not an accident. It is a direct result of the coaching staff's ability to identify specific skills and develop them, combined with a system that rewards effort and role clarity over individual stardom.

The list of notable undrafted Heat players is long and genuinely impressive. Udonis Haslem went undrafted in 2002 and spent twenty seasons with the franchise, winning three championships and becoming one of the most beloved figures in Miami history. Duncan Robinson went undrafted in 2018 and became one of the most efficient three-point shooters in the league within two years. The Heat find players other teams overlook and turn them into pieces that fit.

The reason this works is connected directly to Heat Culture. Undrafted players tend to arrive with something to prove and nothing to lose. They are often more coachable than high draft picks because they have not been told their entire lives that they are special. The Heat take that hunger, give it a structure and a system, and produce players that make other front offices wonder how they missed them. It is one of the more quietly impressive things about the organization.

18. Pat Riley: Suits, Rings, and Thirty Years of Running the Show

Pat Riley has been involved with the Miami Heat as either head coach or team president since 1995. Thirty years. In that time the Heat have won three championships, made six Finals appearances, and developed a reputation as one of the best-run organizations in professional basketball. That does not happen by accident and it does not happen without someone at the top who knows what winning requires.

Riley won four championships coaching the Showtime Lakers in the 1980s. He won another with the Knicks-era toughness approach he refined in New York. He came to Miami and won a sixth as team president in 2006, a seventh in 2012, and an eighth in 2013. Eight championships across multiple decades and multiple organizations. The man knows how to build winning teams.

What makes Riley interesting beyond the trophies is the consistency of his approach. He has never chased trends. When the league went small and pace-heavy, Miami still valued defense and physicality. When other teams rebuilt by tanking, the Heat kept competing. Riley's belief that standards should not change based on circumstances is either stubborn or admirable depending on your perspective. Based on the results, it looks a lot more like admirable. Also his suits genuinely are exceptional. That part is not relevant to winning championships but it is worth mentioning.

19. The Miami Vice Uniforms: Basketball Meets South Beach

In 2018, the Miami Heat unveiled a set of alternate uniforms inspired by the 1980s television show Miami Vice. Pink and blue. Neon colors. A design that looked like it belonged on a yacht at sunset in 1986. The basketball world had opinions immediately and those opinions were mostly very positive.

The Vice uniforms became one of the most popular alternate kits in the league almost immediately. Fans bought them. Players wore them with visible enthusiasm. The pink and blue color scheme showed up on sneakers, accessories, and merchandise that had nothing to do with basketball. Miami leaned into the South Beach identity in a way that felt authentic rather than forced, because South Beach is genuinely that colorful and that distinctive.

The uniforms also worked on the court in a specific way. When Miami was winning in the Vice alternates, the visual of those pink and blue uniforms in a packed arena under bright lights created an atmosphere that felt different from a standard home game. The Heat already had one of the louder home crowds in the East. The Vice nights added a visual element that made the building feel like a different kind of event. Sometimes a uniform is just a uniform. Sometimes it is part of the whole experience.

20. Kaseya Center and South Beach: Location, Location, Location

The Miami Heat play in Kaseya Center, an arena in downtown Miami that opened in 1999 and sits about two miles from South Beach. It holds just under 20,000 fans for basketball games and has been consistently ranked among the better game-day experiences in the NBA. But the building itself is only part of the story. The location is the other part.

There is no other NBA arena quite like this one in terms of what surrounds it. The Miami waterfront is visible from outside the building. South Beach, one of the most famous stretches of real estate in the world, is a short drive away. The city itself brings an energy to game nights that not every NBA market can replicate. When the Heat are playing well, getting a ticket to a game is genuinely difficult, and the atmosphere inside reflects a city that treats its entertainment seriously.

The arena has gone through multiple naming rights sponsors over the years, which is just the nature of arena naming deals in modern sports. It was American Airlines Arena for most of its existence before becoming FTX Arena briefly and then Kaseya Center. The names change. The building stays the same. And on a warm Miami night with a playoff game on the line, there are not many places in the league louder than that corner of downtown. South Beach has a way of showing up when the stakes are high.

21. Erik Spoelstra: The Coach Who Earned Every Bit of It

Erik Spoelstra became the Miami Heat's head coach in 2008 at 37 years old. He had never been a head coach at any level before. He had worked his way up through the Heat organization from video coordinator to assistant coach over more than a decade. Pat Riley hired him and then watched the basketball world immediately wonder whether the choice was too soon, too young, and too inexperienced.

Sixteen seasons later, Spoelstra has three championship rings and has led the Heat to six Finals appearances. He has consistently gotten maximum results from rosters that did not always look like championship caliber on paper. The 2020 bubble run was probably the most impressive coaching job of his career, taking a team without a recognized superstar all the way to the Finals through preparation, system, and player development.

What Spoelstra does exceptionally well is adjust. He is not a coach who finds one system and runs it regardless of his roster. He reshapes his approach based on the players he has, which sounds simple and is actually very difficult to do consistently over a long career. He has coached LeBron James and Dwyane Wade and Bam Adebayo and undrafted rookies, and he has gotten meaningful contributions from all of them. There is an argument that he is among the best coaches in the league right now. There is also an argument that the argument understates the case.

22. Bam Adebayo: The Most Complete Player in Miami Today

Bam Adebayo was drafted fourteenth overall by the Miami Heat in 2017 out of Kentucky. He was known coming in as a defender and rebounder with limited offensive polish. Seven seasons later he is the best player on the team, a four-time All-Star, one of the better defensive centers in the league, and the man who just scored 83 points in a single game. That is a development arc worth paying attention to.

What makes Adebayo valuable on a daily basis, separate from the historic night in March, is his versatility. He can guard point guards on the perimeter and protect the rim in the same possession. He passes out of the high post like a point forward. He screens with purpose. He communicates on defense in a way that makes the whole unit more organized. None of those things show up prominently in a box score, but every coach in the league understands what they are worth.

The 83-point game added a new dimension to how the league thinks about him offensively, though it would be unrealistic to expect that output regularly. What it proved was that the scoring ability was there in a way that had not fully been demonstrated before. Adebayo is 28 years old and under contract in Miami. He is the centerpiece of whatever the Heat build next, and given what this organization has done with centerpieces before, that is a reasonable thing to feel good about.

23. Tyler Herro: The Kid Who Never Stopped Believing

Tyler Herro was drafted 13th overall by Miami in 2019 and almost immediately became polarizing. He was confident in a way that some people found refreshing and others found irritating. He shot the ball in spots that made coaches nervous. He talked like someone who had already proven everything when he had not yet proven anything. Then he scored 37 points off the bench in a playoff game at 20 years old in the 2020 bubble, and the confidence started to look more like self-knowledge than arrogance.

Herro has had a complicated path since that bubble breakout. Injuries slowed him down. His development was not always linear. There were stretches where the Heat tried to trade him for an established star and stretches where he looked like exactly the player they had always hoped he would become. He won the Sixth Man of the Year award in 2022, which validated the role the Heat had built around him as a scorer off the bench who could occasionally start when needed.

He is currently 26 years old and one of Miami's primary offensive weapons. He can shoot off the dribble, create his own shot, and score in bunches on nights when his rhythm is right. The Heat have built their offensive identity around spacing and movement, and Herro fits that identity well. Whether he becomes a cornerstone or a complementary piece in the next great Heat team is still being written. Either way, the kid who never stopped believing is still here.

24. Life After Jimmy: A New Chapter Begins

Jimmy Butler spent five and a half seasons with the Miami Heat and his time there was almost never boring. He led the 2020 bubble run almost single-handedly. He was one of the most competitive players in the league during his Miami years, a player who saved his best performances for the biggest games and wore his intensity like a uniform. He also had a complicated relationship with the organization that eventually ran its course.

In February 2025, the Heat traded Butler to the Golden State Warriors. The circumstances of the departure were messy and involved suspensions and standoffs that filled sports columns for months. What the Heat got back in return was draft capital, including the pick that became Kasparas Jakucionis, a 20-year-old Lithuanian guard with genuine playmaking ability who is now getting his first real NBA minutes.

The Heat are 38 and 29 this season without Butler, which suggests the roster is more resilient than some expected after losing their most prominent player. Adebayo is the anchor. Herro is the scorer. Spoelstra is the coach. The young pieces around them are developing. Miami has been through bigger transitions than this and come out the other side in better shape. The Heat losing a star and rebuilding quietly into something competitive again is actually a fairly familiar story. They have done it before.

25. The Heat Never Cool Down

The Miami Heat have been an NBA franchise since 1988. In that time they have won three championships, made six Finals appearances, and produced some of the most memorable moments in league history. For a franchise that started from nothing with fifteen wins in its first season, that is a remarkable amount of ground covered in less than four decades.

What makes Miami's story worth following into the future is the stability underneath the star power. Other franchises rise and fall based entirely on whether a superstar wants to be there. The Heat rise and fall too, but they always seem to find their footing faster than most. The coaching staff stays intact. The culture stays consistent. The player development pipeline keeps producing. Those things matter more over time than any single player's decision to come or go.

The current team has Bam Adebayo in his prime, Tyler Herro still developing, a young draft pick in Jakucionis just beginning his story, and Erik Spoelstra drawing up a game plan that will give all of them the best chance to succeed. South Beach has seen a lot of great basketball over the years. The next chapter is still blank. But if you have been paying attention to how this organization operates, you already know they will fill it with something worth watching. The Heat do not stay cold for long. They never have.

Bonus Trivia Quiz!

You think you are a true Heat fan? Try this bonus quiz!

1. How many games did the Miami Heat win in their very first NBA season?

A) 15
B) 22
C) 28
D) 31

2. Pat Riley won four championships as a coach with which team before coming to Miami?

A) Boston Celtics
B) Chicago Bulls
C) Los Angeles Lakers
D) New York Knicks

3. Dwyane Wade was drafted by Miami with which pick in the 2003 NBA Draft?

A) 1st
B) 3rd
C) 5th
D) 8th

4. How many points did Dwyane Wade average per game in the final four games of the 2006 NBA Finals?

A) 26.2

B) 29.8

C) 32.1

D) 34.7

5. Which team did the Miami Heat defeat to win the 2013 NBA Championship?

A) Oklahoma City Thunder

B) Indiana Pacers

C) San Antonio Spurs

D) Dallas Mavericks

6. How old was Ray Allen when he hit the corner three to tie Game 6 of the 2013 Finals?

A) 33

B) 35

C) 37

D) 39

7. Udonis Haslem spent how many seasons with the Miami Heat?

A) 12
B) 15
C) 18
D) 20

8. Tyler Herro scored 37 points off the bench during which playoff series in the 2020 bubble?

A) First Round vs. Indiana
B) Second Round vs. Milwaukee
C) Eastern Conference Finals vs. Boston
D) NBA Finals vs. Los Angeles

9. How many points did Bam Adebayo score in his record-breaking game against the Washington Wizards in March 2026?

A) 75
B) 79
C) 81
D) 83

10. What was the name of the popular alternate uniforms the Heat introduced in 2018?

A) South Beach Edition
B) Miami Vice uniforms
C) Sunset Series
D) Neon Nights uniforms

11. Which award did Tyler Herro win in the 2021-22 NBA season?

A) Most Improved Player
B) Defensive Player of the Year
C) Sixth Man of the Year
D) Rookie of the Year

12. How old was Erik Spoelstra when he became head coach of the Miami Heat?

A) 33
B) 35
C) 37
D) 40

13. Alonzo Mourning was diagnosed with which serious condition that threatened his career?

A) A heart condition
B) A kidney disease
C) A lung condition
D) A spinal injury

14. The Miami Heat paid how much for their NBA expansion franchise in 1988?

A) 12.5 million dollars
B) 20 million dollars
C) 32.5 million dollars
D) 45 million dollars

15. Which young Lithuanian guard did the Heat select with their 2025 first-round draft pick?

A) Nolan Traoré
B) Egor Demin
C) Ben Saraf
D) Kasparas Jakucionis

Super Fan Secret Challenge

Only a true Heat fan will know this.

(No Answer Provided)

The Miami Heat made a stunning run to the NBA Finals in the 2020 bubble without a single player who had been an All-Star that season. They were led by a player who averaged 26 points per game in the bubble playoffs and played like someone who had been waiting his whole career for that moment. He did not win a championship that year, but he made sure everyone knew his name. Who was that player, how many points did he average in the 2020 bubble playoffs, and which team ultimately beat the Heat in the Finals?

Answer Key

1. A) 15

2. C) Los Angeles Lakers

3. C) 5th

4. D) 34.7

5. C) San Antonio Spurs

6. C) 37

7. D) 20

8. C) Eastern Conference Finals vs. Boston

9. D) 83

10. B) Miami Vice uniforms

11. C) Sixth Man of the Year

12. C) 37

13. B) A kidney disease

14. C) 32.5 million dollars

15. D) Kasparas Jakucionis

NBA PLAYOFF BRACKET

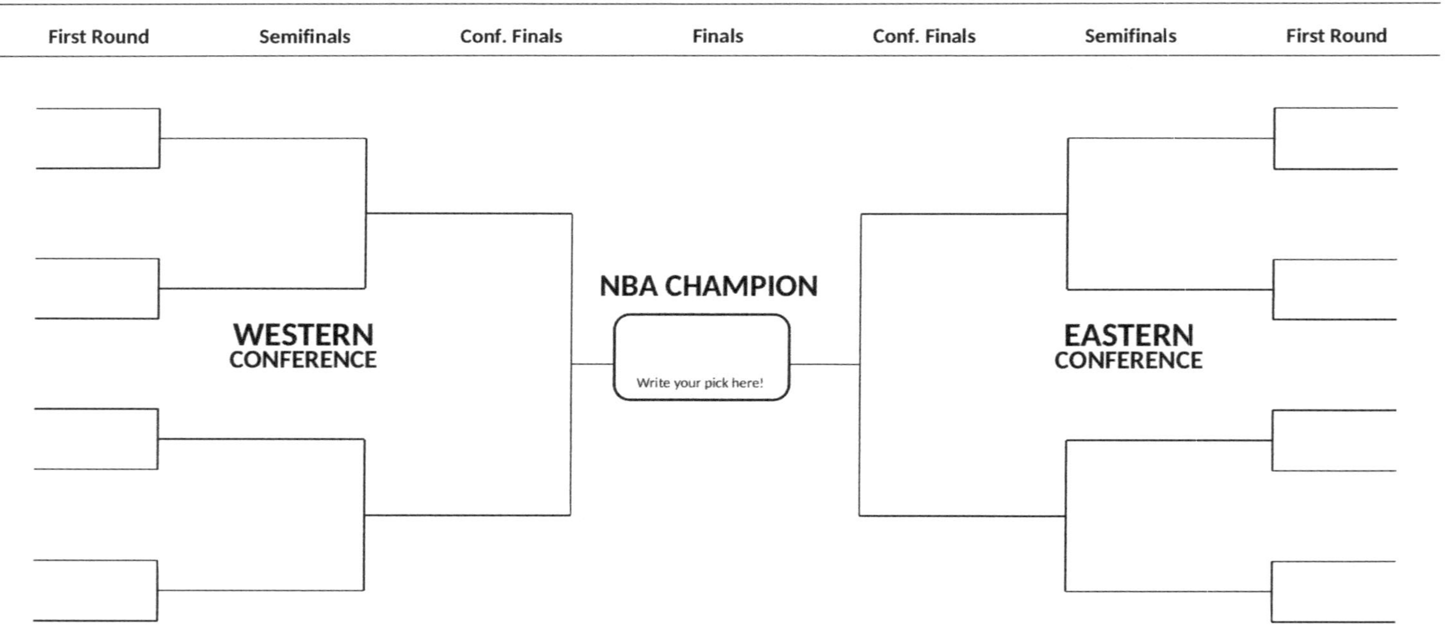

* Fill in your picks and try not to argue with your friends about it!

Part of the Fun Fan Facts: The Unofficial Sports Guide Series

Be the Boss of the Playoffs

You've broken down the matchups. You know which superstar takes over in the fourth quarter. You've seen the bench units that quietly decide series. You've watched the adjustments coaches make when their backs are against the wall.

Now it's time to stop watching and start deciding.

On this page, you are not just a fan. You are the Head Coach drawing up the last play with three seconds left on the clock. You are the GM who built this roster. You are the analyst who saw it all coming.

This is not just filling out a bracket.

This is building your championship run.

Sixteen teams enter the NBA Playoffs. The path is brutal. Best of seven. No shortcuts. No hiding. Every round gets louder, harder, and more personal.

This bracket is your Playoff Control Room.

The Game Plan

1. Survive Round One: Start with the opening round. Which matchup is going seven games? Who has the closer? Who folds under pressure? Make the calls.

2. Feel the Momentum: As you move into the Conference Semifinals and Conference Finals, things change. Role players become heroes. Stars feel the weight. Trust your reads.

3. Own the Finals: Trace your picks all the way to the NBA Finals. When the confetti falls and the trophy is raised, you'll find out who earned it.

House Rules: Circle your boldest upset. That is your official "I knew it" moment.

Choose Your Weapon: Pencil if you want flexibility. Pen if you trust your instincts. Sharpie if you believe in chaos.

Because once the playoffs tip off, there is no rewinding Game 7.

Make your picks. Trust your basketball brain. And let the playoff drama begin.

Fun Facts Wrap-Up

You made it through! You're officially a true superfan! Now it's time to put your knowledge to the test. Share these facts with friends and see who really knows their team best.

Love the series?

Your reviews help other fans discover Fun Fan Facts. If you enjoyed this book, we'd really appreciate you sharing your thoughts and leaving a review.

Want more Fun Fan Facts?

Scan the QR code below to visit our site and explore bonus trivia, challenges, and special extras - including new teams, future series, and collectible fun as they're released.

Collect All the Fun Fan Facts Series!

Check off every book you read. See the full set on Amazon. Search "Fun Fan Facts Jake Liam."

World Cup 2026 Edition

☐ Algeria	☐ Scotland	☐ Morocco
☐ France	☐ Brazil	☐ Switzerland
☐ Paraguay	☐ Ivory Coast	☐ Curaçao
☐ Argentina	☐ Senegal	☐ Netherlands
☐ Germany	☐ Canada	☐ Tunisia
☐ Portugal	☐ Japan	☐ Ecuador
☐ Australia	☐ South Africa	☐ New Zealand
☐ Ghana	☐ Cape Verde	☐ United States
☐ Qatar	☐ Jordan	☐ Egypt
☐ Austria	☐ South Korea	☐ Norway
☐ Haiti	☐ Colombia	☐ Uruguay
☐ Saudi Arabia	☐ Mexico	☐ England
☐ Belgium	☐ Spain	☐ Panama
☐ Iran	☐ Croatia	☐ Uzbekistan

World Cup 2026 Group Edition

☐ Group A	☐ Group F	☐ Group K
☐ Group E	☐ Group J	☐ Group D
☐ Group I	☐ Group C	☐ Group H
☐ Group B	☐ Group G	☐ Group L

English Football Edition

- ☐ Arsenal F.C.
- ☐ Aston Villa F.C.
- ☐ Chelsea F.C.
- ☐ Everton F.C.
- ☐ Fulham F.C.
- ☐ Liverpool F.C.
- ☐ Manchester City
- ☐ Manchester United
- ☐ Newcastle United F.C.
- ☐ Tottenham Hotspur
- ☐ West Ham United
- ☐ Wrexham A.F.C.

NBA Edition

- ☐ Atlanta Hawks
- ☐ Boston Celtics
- ☐ Brooklyn Nets
- ☐ Charlotte Hornets
- ☐ Chicago Bulls
- ☐ Cleveland Cavaliers
- ☐ Dallas Mavericks
- ☐ Denver Nuggets
- ☐ Detroit Pistons
- ☐ Golden State Warriors
- ☐ Houston Rockets
- ☐ Indiana Pacers
- ☐ LA Clippers
- ☐ Los Angeles Lakers
- ☐ Memphis Grizzlies
- ☐ Miami Heat
- ☐ Milwaukee Bucks
- ☐ Minnesota Timberwolves
- ☐ New Orleans Pelicans
- ☐ New York Knicks
- ☐ Oklahoma City Thunder
- ☐ Orlando Magic
- ☐ Philadelphia 76ers
- ☐ Phoenix Suns
- ☐ Portland Trail Blazers
- ☐ Sacramento Kings
- ☐ San Antonio Spurs
- ☐ Toronto Raptors
- ☐ Utah Jazz
- ☐ Washington Wizards

About the Author

Jake is a 13-year-old sports fan who loves football, American football, and basketball. He plays soccer as a goalie and dreams of one day playing for West Ham United and helping teach kids to love the game. His passion for sports runs in the family - his dad was a professional baseball player, and his stepdad sparked his love for West Ham. Through the Fun Fan Facts series, he shares the fun and excitement of sports with fans everywhere.

www.ingramcontent.com/pod-product-compliance
Lightning Source LLC
Chambersburg PA
CBHW050043040726
47599CB00015B/1777